OWLS

Who Gives a Hoot?

FRANCES BACKHOUSE

ORCA BOOK PUBLISHERS

Published in Canada and the United States
in 2024 by Orca Book Publishers.
orcabook.com

Library and Archives Canada Cataloguing in Publication
Title: Owls : who gives a hoot? / Frances Backhouse.
Names: Backhouse, Frances, author.
Series: Orca wild ; 13.
Description: Series statement: Orca wild ; 13 |
Includes bibliographical references and index.
Identifiers: Canadiana (print) 20230472710 |
Canadiana (ebook) 20230472729 | ISBN 9781459835290 (hardcover) |
ISBN 9781459835306 (PDF) | ISBN 9781459835313 (EPUB)
Subjects: LCSH: Owls—North America—Juvenile literature. |
LCSH: Owls—Behavior—Juvenile literature. |
LCSH: Owls—Conservation—Juvenile literature.
Classification: LCC QL696.S8 B33 2024 | DDC j598.9/7097—dc23

Library of Congress Control Number: 2023942212

Summary: Part of the nonfiction Orca Wild series for middle-grade
readers and illustrated with color photographs throughout, this book
introduces kids to owls in North America. It discusses owl habitat,
biology and threats to survival, and how scientists, conservationists
and young people are working to protect owls everywhere.

Orca Book Publishers is committed to reducing the consumption of
nonrenewable resources in the production of our books. We make
every effort to use materials that support a sustainable future.

Orca Book Publishers gratefully acknowledges the support
for its publishing programs provided by the following
agencies: the Government of Canada, the Canada Council for
the Arts and the Province of British Columbia through the
BC Arts Council and the Book Publishing Tax Credit.

Front cover photo by lavin photography/Getty Images
Back cover photo by Daniel Garrido/Getty Images
Design by Jenn Playford and Dahlia Yuen
Edited by Kirstie Hudson

Printed and bound in South Korea.

27 26 25 24 • 1 2 3 4

A short-eared owl cruises over a field.
CARLDAYPHOTOGRAPHY/GETTY IMAGES

For Helen and John, the wise owls who nurtured me and showed me how to fly.
And for Cordelia, the littlest chick in my family's nest.

Contents

2 Stealthy Hunters

1 Getting Acquainted

3 Owl Life

4 Giving a Hoot

The barred owl is named for the horizontal stripes that run down its chest and belly. Its dark brown eyes and yellow bill are also helpful clues to its identity.
©JARED HOBBS

Introduction

In spring I often sleep with my bedroom window open. Some nights I'm jolted awake by hollering outside my house. It sounds like someone gargling, laughing, yelling and being strangled all at once.

I don't worry though. I know it's only a pair of barred owls having a conversation. Their crazy calling tells me they're planning to nest nearby. Hello neighbors, I think. And once they quiet down, I roll over and go back to sleep.

A lot of encounters with owls are like that—just a voice in the night. That makes seeing one of these mysterious birds all the more special.

Usually when I see owls they are half-hidden in the branches of a tree or only shadowy figures in the dark. When I do manage to get a good look, and they look back, I am struck by how expressive their faces seem and the direct way they meet my gaze.

Here I am with a northern saw-whet owl.
As these owls travel south in the fall, biologists
capture them to gather information that will help
protect them. After a short delay, the owls are
set free to continue their journey.
VICKY YOUNG

Once, I got to hold an owl in my hands. It was a clear, cold night in the middle of October, and I was helping with a study of northern saw-whet owls. The researchers caught the owls in nets strung up between trees and then took them to their workstation—a simple shelter with plastic walls that rattled in the wind.

Sitting at a workbench full of scientific equipment, one person examined, weighed and measured each owl before slipping an identification band around one of its legs. Another person recorded the data. This skilled work had to be done quickly and carefully, so mostly I just watched. But they did let me launch one of the owls.

First we walked well away from the lighted shelter and let the darkness wrap around us. When the man who was carrying the owl handed it to me, I grasped its feather-covered legs with one hand and cupped my other hand behind its back. It felt incredibly soft against my bare skin.

The owl must have been afraid, but it didn't struggle, just stared at me with huge golden eyes. For a moment I gazed back. Then I unfurled my fingers from its legs, and with a silent flutter of wings it was gone.

I was already interested in owls before that evening. By the end of it, I was a dedicated fan. Now whenever I'm someplace where there might be owls, I listen and look for them. And I love learning about them. I hope you do too.

Twelve-year-old Greysen Jakes holds a northern saw-whet owl at the Owl Research Institute field station in Montana. During his night at the station, Greysen learned how to catch and safely handle owls and helped the researchers take measurements.
ANDREW JAKES

A northern saw-whet owl.
JACKVANDENHEUVEL/GETTY IMAGES

A barn owl surveys its surroundings from the window of an old barn. Barn owls have very long legs, which help them snatch prey from tall grass.
JOSEPH VAN OS/GETTY IMAGES

1

Getting Acquainted

OWLS EVERYWHERE

If you know where to look, you can find owls almost anywhere you go in the world. They live on every continent except Antarctica and on most major islands. Owls make their homes in all kinds of places, including forests, grasslands, deserts, jungles, mountains and cities. Some are comfortable in cold and snow. Others prefer tropical heat. Many choose something in between.

How many different kinds of owls are there? Even the experts can't agree on an exact number. Biologists separate them into *species* based on what they look like and how they behave. Owls that belong to the same species are close relatives and can mate with each other. But some owls are so rare or secretive it's hard to figure out who they are related to. Even common owls can be confusing. Every now and then new research shows that one species should be split into two, or two species should be combined into one. The owls are still the same birds, but their official names are changed.

For now we can say that there are about 250 owl species worldwide. No one person has ever seen all of them. Maybe you could be the first to achieve that goal!

You could start by setting out to see all the owl species that live in Canada and the United States. After all, there are only 19. And no matter which state, province or territory you are in, you share that place with at least two different kinds of owls.

A western screech-owl stands guard at the entrance to its nest hole. Its camouflage coloring and markings blend in with the tree bark and help it hide from enemies.
©JARED HOBBS

WHO'S WHOO

North America's 19 owl species are:

barn owl

barred owl

boreal owl

burrowing owl

eastern screech-owl

elf owl

ferruginous pygmy-owl

flammulated owl

great gray owl

great horned owl

long-eared owl

northern hawk owl

northern pygmy-owl

northern saw-whet owl

short-eared owl

snowy owl

spotted owl

western screech-owl

whiskered screech-owl

IN ORDER OF APPEARANCE
ROW 1: JOSEPH VAN OS/GETTY IMAGES; MIKESPICS/GETTY IMAGES; NPS/PUBLIC DOMAIN; NPS/DORI: SCOTT SURIANO/GETTY IMAGES
ROW 2: ROLF NUSSBAUMER/GETTY IMAGES; STAN TEKIELA/GETTY IMAGES; ©JARED HOBBS; VISHAL SUBRAMANYAN (2)
ROW 3: RUSSELL BURDEN/GETTY IMAGES; NPS/EMILY MESNER; ©JARED HOBBS; TOM WALKER/GETTY IMAGES; NPS/PUBLIC DOMAIN
ROW 4: ©JARED HOBBS (4)

HEY, I KNOW YOU

Owls aren't the easiest birds to spot, but if you get a good look, they are easy to recognize. Of course, it takes some skill and practice to learn to tell which species is which. But whether it's a Javan owlet in Indonesia, an Itombwe owl in central Africa or a great horned owl in your backyard, the basic features of all owls are the same. They include:

an upright posture

JAMESVANCOUVER/GETTY IMAGES

a compact body and large head

MARTIN-KUBIK/GETTY IMAGES

a small down-curved bill

DETLEF KNAPP/GETTY IMAGES

big forward-facing eyes

JILLLANG/GETTY IMAGES

powerful feet with sharp talons

GARYTOG/GETTY

Another thing all owls have in common is that they are never colorful. No flashy red, green, purple or blue feathers for these birds. They stick to shades of brown, black, gray and white. The only bright touches that some owls have are yellow or orange eyes, bills or feet.

Owls have poor color vision, so there's no point dressing up for each other in eye-catching attire. It's more important for them to be hard to see in the daytime, when most of them sleep. Their dull coloring helps owls hide in shadows and blend in with their surroundings. Patterns created by spots, streaks, blotches, bars and other markings add to the camouflage effect.

In most owl species, females and males have identical *plumage*. Snowy owls are one of the few exceptions, but the differences between males and females are not clear-cut. Some snowy owls are pure white. Others are spattered with gray and brown markings. Young males and adult females typically have the most markings, but some females are as white as the whitest males.

Snowy owls are North America's heaviest owls, followed by great horned owls and great gray owls. Great grays are tops in terms of body length and wingspan. Their thick, fluffy plumage makes great gray owls look bigger than great horned owls, but they actually weigh about 15 percent less.

NIGHTTIME, DAYTIME, IN-BETWEEN TIME

Owls are best known for being active after dark, but not all owls are night owls. Different species have different activity patterns.

Nocturnal owls generally conduct their business at night and sleep during the day.

Crepuscular owls also sleep during the day and are most active during the twilight period around dusk and dawn.

Diurnal owls are active during the day and sleep at night.

These categories aren't strict rules for owl behavior. Sometimes owls need to be active outside of their usual hours. This often happens during the breeding season, as owl parents work overtime to get enough food for themselves and their families. Owls also spend more time hunting when there are prey shortages or when bad weather makes it hard to get enough to eat. Activity patterns are also more variable in the far north, where summer nights are very short and winter nights are very long. Northern owls are good at operating in either daylight or darkness.

No matter when they sleep, owls never sleep deeply. They remain alert and frequently open their eyes to scan their surroundings. Their quiet time—either sleeping or resting—is called *roosting*. The place where they sleep or rest is called a *roost*. Owls choose roosts where they will be hidden from enemies and protected from rain, snow, cold winds and hot sun. That might be deep within the branches of a bushy evergreen tree, inside a cozy tree-trunk hole or on a sheltered cliff ledge. Each species has its favorite roost sites. So do individual owls.

Northern saw-whet owls often roost in large evergreen trees, sheltered by overhanging branches. In winter these owls usually roost in the same place every day for weeks or months.
BOB HILSCHER/GETTY IMAGES

WHO'S WHOO

©JARED HOBBS

Elf Owl

Elf owls live in deserts and other dry habitats. They mainly eat insects that they catch in flight or pluck off the ground. Sometimes they hunt around outdoor lights, like bats do. They also hang from flowers or leaves and probe for prey. These sparrow-sized owls nest in woodpecker holes in cactuses and trees. Most elf owls breed in three separate areas that span the United States–Mexico border and spend winters farther south in Mexico. Some live in Mexico year-round.

MINIS AND GIANTS

Owls come in all sizes. The world's smallest owl is the elf owl. The largest is Blakiston's fish owl. Elf owls live in the southwestern United States and the northern half of Mexico. These tiny birds stand less than 6 inches (15 centimeters) tall and weigh 1.3 to 1.7 ounces (37 to 48 grams). That's about the same weight as a golf ball. With their short tails and compact bodies, they are about the size and shape of a soda can.

You could cup an elf owl in the palm of your hand, but you would need to use two arms to hold a Blakiston's fish owl. These giants stand about 2.5 feet (76 centimeters) tall and weigh 7.5 to 11 pounds (3.4 to 5.1 kilograms). When they fly, their outspread wings measure about 6 feet (1.8 meters) from tip to tip. Blakiston's fish owls are mainly found in eastern Russia and northern Japan. They are in trouble because people are cutting down too much of the forests where they live and catching too many of the fish they depend on for food. Altogether, fewer than 2,000 of these magnificent owls remain.

Biologist Jonathan Slaght with a Blakiston's fish owl in eastern Russia. His research team caught it to learn more about this species and help protect it. Before releasing the owl, they fed it a few fish, like the trout gripped in its bill.
SERGEI AVDEYUK/COURTESY OF JONATHAN C. SLAGHT

Female owls are usually larger than males. In many species there is only a small size difference, but female boreal owls can be as much as 40 percent heavier than males. The burrowing owl is the only North American species in which males are slightly bigger than females.

A pair of northern hawk owls. The female, sitting closest to the tree trunk, is a bit bigger than the male.
RON HOETMER/GETTY IMAGES

A Blakiston's fish owl intent on catching a fish plunges into an icy pool in a river in Japan.

The Ainu are the Indigenous People of northern Japan. Their name for Blakiston's fish owl is Kotan-kor-kamuy, which means God of the Village. In Ainu tradition, Kotan-kor-kamuy is a sacred bird that protects villagers from starvation. Now it is people who must protect the owls. Forty years ago there were very few Blakiston's fish owls left in Japan. Since then their numbers have doubled, thanks to focused *conservation* efforts.

ANCIENT STORIES AND BELIEFS

Japan is not the only place where owls are part of traditional teachings. All around the world, no other group of birds has inspired so many stories and beliefs.

Owls are often regarded as spooky or scary. That's because most owls are creatures of the night, and many people don't feel at ease in the dark. Throughout history humans have tended to view night as a time of danger, death and evil. As a result, many cultures connect owls

with these things. Traditions that say owls warn of death or misfortune exist on every continent. Beliefs linking owls to ghosts, witches and demons are also widespread.

But sometimes owls are seen as powerful animals that do good things for people, like the Ainu god Kotan-kor-kamuy. In ancient Greece owls were associated with Athena, the goddess of wisdom. That link between wisdom and owls has carried down through the centuries in many cultures with European roots.

Indigenous Peoples in North America have many different traditional beliefs about owls. For example, in Alutiiq tradition owls are spiritual helpers for shamans. One Ojibwe-Anishinaabeg teaching about owls is that Gookooko'oo, the spirit who represents all owls, assists people on their way to the Spirit World. Gookooko'oo can also be an individual's guardian spirit.

An Alutiiq artist in Alaska carved this wooden mask long ago. It represents the face of a short-eared owl.
OWL MASK, KARLUK ONE (AM193), KONIAG INC. COLLECTION, COURTESY ALUTIIQ MUSEUM AND ARCHAEOLOGICAL REPOSITORY

Eight-year-old Stella Green is ready to go trick-or-treating dressed up as a snowy owl—her favorite kind of owl. In the summer Stella set up a lemonade stand and donated the money she made to the Owl Research Institute's snowy owl research project.

ADAM GREEN

IMAGINING OWLS TODAY

Owls still have a strong hold on our imaginations. Think of all the owl decorations you see at Halloween. Or the wise-owl images that are so common on school graduation cards and library posters.

The author J.K. Rowling chose owls to be messengers in her Harry Potter stories because of their reputation as magical animals. Since they are fictional characters, they don't always behave like real owls, but Rowling modeled them on real species. The Weasley family has Errol, a great gray owl. Draco Malfoy's unnamed owl is a Eurasian eagle-owl. And Harry's owl, Hedwig, is a snowy owl. Even though Hedwig is female, the animal actors that portray her in the movies are all males, chosen for their pure-white plumage.

HOME SWEET HABITAT

In the everyday world we have no reason to fear owls, but they have reasons to fear us. Human activities threaten owls in a number of ways. The biggest problem for many species is that they are losing their *habitat*—the place where they live and can find food, cover and all the other things they need to survive.

Many of the world's owls live in forests. If this habitat is logged, they are left homeless. It's like having someone barge into your house and trash your bedroom, kitchen, dining room and living room. But it's much harder to fix a damaged or destroyed forest. Growing big trees takes anywhere from many decades to a few centuries.

Owls that live in wide-open grasslands, such as short-eared owls and burrowing owls, are also at risk. They lose their habitat when people plow up land to grow crops or cover it with roads and buildings.

Species that use a wide variety of habitats, such as the great horned owl, can put up with quite a bit of human disruption. But species that can only live in one particular type of habitat aren't so adaptable. If their habitat disappears, so do these habitat specialists.

WHO'S WHOO

JOSEPH VAN OS/GETTY IMAGES

Barn Owl

Barn owls are found around the world and are the most widespread of all owl species. They live in open habitats in many parts of the United States and along the southern edges of British Columbia and Ontario. These medium-sized owls nest in many kinds of holes, such as nooks in barns and hollows in tree trunks. They are rarely seen in action because they are strictly nocturnal. Barn owls can locate prey by sound alone more accurately than any other animal that has been tested.

WHO'S WHOO

Spotted Owl

These medium-sized owls are mainly nocturnal. They are found from southern British Columbia to southern California, in the southwestern United States and in north and central Mexico. They mostly live in old-growth forests, but in the southwestern states and Mexico they sometimes live in narrow canyons with few trees. In the northern part of their range, spotted owls have dark-brown plumage dotted with small white markings. In the southern part, they are lighter brown with larger spots.

NOWHERE TO GO

One habitat specialist is the spotted owl. In most parts of their *range*, spotted owls depend on *old-growth forest* habitats. There they can find large trees with roomy holes and hollows in their trunks for nest sites. The thick branches near the treetops offer cool shade during hot weather and dry shelter when it's rainy. Old-growth forests are also full of spotted owl prey, including flying squirrels and wood rats. And the owls can easily zip between the trunks as they hunt because the trees aren't crowded close together.

Spotted owls are becoming scarce in many areas because logging is taking a heavy toll on old-growth forests. They are listed as a threatened species in Mexico and the United States and are one of Canada's most endangered animals, found only in British Columbia. This province was once home to about 1,000 spotted owls. Now just a handful remain.

DEADLY COLLISIONS

Some human dangers come at owls at high speed. Owls are often drawn to roadsides because they are good places to find rodents and other prey. But hunting close to roads is highly hazardous, especially at night. Every year thousands of owls are struck by vehicles and killed or injured. It's hard for drivers to see owls in time to avoid hitting them. And a hungry owl may be too focused on getting a meal to notice oncoming traffic. The faster a car is moving, the less time an owl has to dodge it.

Some kinds of owls are at risk of being hit because they cruise close to the ground when hunting. These low fliers include short-eared owls and barn owls. Many other owl species hunt from perches. They may be struck as they

A great gray owl lies dead on the road after being hit by a car. The best way for drivers to avoid this kind of tragic accident is to slow down when traveling in areas where wildlife is common. VISHAL SUBRAMANYAN

swoop down to catch prey on the ground or slowly take off carrying a heavy load.

Collision with a vehicle is a common cause of death for burrowing owls because they often walk, hop or run after their prey. In summer they mainly eat *invertebrates*, such as scorpions, beetles and crickets. In winter they focus on small mammals and birds. All of these animals are abundant along roads. Unfortunately, the number of busy roads cutting through burrowing owl habitat is increasing.

Airports are also danger zones. Airplanes regularly collide with short-eared owls and snowy owls as they hunt in the open fields around landing strips. Occasionally the birds are sucked into a plane's engine. In addition to killing or injuring the owls, these accidents can damage the airplanes.

Long-eared owls are more sociable than most owls. They sometimes nest close together and hunt in the same places as their neighbors. In winter they regularly roost in groups, often perched just a few body lengths apart. One roosting site may have up to 100 owls, but 2 to 20 is more common.

Elsa Jehle stands near a long-eared-owl winter roost in Montana with an owl she helped a research crew flush out of this thicket and into a net. The crew has measured and banded the owl. Now Elsa will release it.

ALEX JEHLE

POISON PERILS

It's hard to imagine anyone poisoning owls on purpose, but people often poison them by accident. This happens when owls eat poisoned prey such as rats, mice and other rodents.

Rodent poisons kill by causing unstoppable bleeding inside the victim's body. It usually takes several days for rodents to die after they eat poison bait. During that time they move around in a dazed and weakened state. That makes them easy targets for owls and other predators, including hawks, foxes, coyotes and pet cats. If the dying rodent gets caught and eaten, the poison carries on working in the predator's body.

Eating poisoned prey is often a death sentence for owls. One bad meal might not kill an owl immediately, but the poison stays in its body and keeps building up as the bird eats more poisoned rodents. Over time the owl's health gets worse. Eventually it may die.

WHY OWLS MATTER

The expression "Out of sight, out of mind" describes a common attitude toward owls. Most people don't give much thought to nighttime birds that hide away during the day. They may not even realize there are owls living nearby or notice if they disappear. But owls are important to all of us, whether we are aware of them or not.

One obvious reason to appreciate owls is that they are fantastic pest controllers. Owls gobble up huge numbers of the kinds of rodents that damage crops, eat stored food and spread diseases. They help safeguard our food supplies and protect our health, and they never send us a bill for their work.

As predators, owls also help keep their whole natural community—or *ecosystem*—healthy and balanced. Ecosystems are held together by food chains that link plants to herbivores (animals that eat plants) and herbivores to predators (animals that eat other animals). The number of predators in an ecosystem is small compared to the number of herbivores and plants, so every one of those predators makes a big contribution to ecosystem health.

Besides these practical values, owls matter to many people because they are so mysterious and magical. When you hear an unseen owl calling in the dark, or you lock eyes with one during a daytime encounter, you get to experience that magic firsthand.

IN SEARCH OF OWLS

Going out in search of owls is called owling. People who go owling are known as owlers. If you're a night owl—a person who likes to stay up late—nighttime owling could be the perfect activity for you. But don't worry if you would rather be in bed in the middle of the night. Some of the best owling opportunities are during the first hour or so after sunset. That's when nocturnal owls wake up from their daytime sleep feeling hungry for breakfast. You also have a good chance of seeing them shortly before sunrise, when they are making their final hunting rounds. Dusk and dawn are excellent times to look for short-eared owls and burrowing owls. Both of these species may be active at any time of day or night, but they favor the twilight hours.

You can even go owling in broad daylight. One species you might spot then is the northern pygmy-owl. These owls commonly hunt during the day and often perch in full

When this great horned owl got stuck in a chicken coop, the farmer called in two experienced owl handlers—Leeza Chamberland and her father. Leeza went into the coop and netted the owl. It had banged its beak trying to escape before they arrived but was in good shape to go free.
RICHARD CHAMBERLAND

WHO'S WHOO

ANNE ELLIOTT/FLICKR.COM

Pygmy-Owls

There are two pygmy-owl species in North America. Northern pygmy-owls live in western Canada, the western United States, Mexico and Central America. Ferruginous pygmy-owls live in South and Central America and a few places in southern Arizona and Texas. Both may be active during the day or around dusk and dawn. These small owls can be identified by the eyespots on the backs of their heads—two large black ovals outlined in white. When other birds mob pygmy-owls, they avoid these false eyes, which are bigger than the owl's real eyes. This reduces the owl's risk of being injured or killed by an attack from behind.

ANNE ELLIOTT/FLICKR.COM

view on poles, trees or power lines when scouting for prey. They like to visit yards with bird feeders to snatch small birds and squirrels.

The northern hawk owl is North America's most diurnal owl species, but it mostly lives far from towns and cities, so not many people see it. Northern hawk owls do nearly all of their hunting when the sun is up. Their preferred place for daytime perching is out in the open, on top of a dead tree.

A MOB OF SPIES

When it comes to finding owls roosting during the day, experienced owlers often count on winged spies to tell them where to look. These spies are birds that don't like having owls around because they are afraid they will get eaten. If they discover an owl's hiding place, they pester it with noisy calls and dive-bombing attacks. This behavior is called *mobbing*. Other birds notice the hullabaloo and join in.

Small birds usually keep their distance when mobbing, and the owl just hunkers down and tries to ignore them. But larger birds are bolder and may strike with their beaks. Gangs of crows often aggressively chase great horned owls from tree to tree while cawing loudly. Jays occasionally kill pygmy-owls. Getting mobbed is no fun for owls, but for owlers it's a great cue that it's time for some owling.

A flock of crows mobs a fleeing great horned owl.
JIM WILLIAMS/GETTY IMAGES

OWL ALLIES

Building for Barn Owls

LAURA DRAKE, GSGLA TROOP 546 LEADER

THOMAS MUSSER

The members of Girl Scout Troop 546 in Santa Clarita, California, care a lot about animals. So when they were picking a project for their Bronze Award, they wanted to do something to help local wildlife. After a conversation with Santa Clarita parks staff, they decided to build homes for barn owls. As Santa Clarita grows, barn owls are being pushed out. Their habitat is also threatened outside the city by wildfires that are getting worse with climate change. But city parks can provide a refuge for barn owls—as long as they have places to nest and roost.

The girls began by studying building plans for barn-owl boxes and figuring out what materials they needed. They raised money to pay for the lumber and other supplies by selling Girl Scout cookies. On construction day everyone gathered at the house of one of the troop members whose father is a skilled woodworker. He had sawed up the planks ahead of time. The Scouts did everything else. Working in pairs, they put the pieces together with screws, wood glue and just a bit of adult assistance.

"I liked thinking about making the barn owls safe while I was making the boxes," Emma Drake says. "I felt good about myself because I felt like I was doing good in the world. And I really liked using power tools and glue and working with wood." By the end of the afternoon, they had six beautifully built boxes. When the troop delivered them to the parks department, their donation doubled the accommodations available for barn owls in Santa Clarita.

A western screech-owl listens for small animals moving about in the night. These owls mostly hunt from perches, sitting and waiting for prey to come into range on the ground below.

2

Stealthy Hunters

RAPTORS THAT RULE THE NIGHT

Owls belong to a group of birds known as *raptors*, or birds of prey. Other raptors include eagles, hawks and falcons. From head to toe, owls are superbly designed for hunting and killing. They have strong, knife-sharp *talons* and sturdy, hooked bills with edges that cut like a razor. This kind of equipment is standard for raptors.

Owls also have some special features that allow them to operate skillfully in the dark, when other raptors are sleeping. Their eyes, ears and flight feathers let owls carry out all kinds of activities at night—not just hunting but also finding nest sites, defending territories, meeting mates and raising families. They can also do these things easily in daylight.

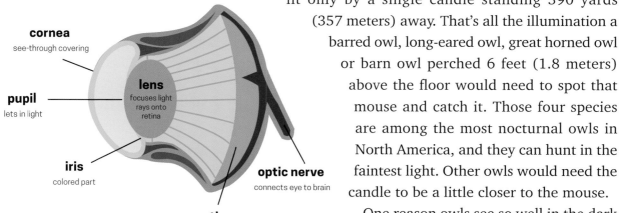

cornea
see-through covering

lens
focuses light rays onto retina

pupil
lets in light

iris
colored part

optic nerve
connects eye to brain

retina
receives light and turns it into electrical signals

A cross-section view of an owl's eye.

ADAPTED FROM OWLPAGES.COM

I SPY WITH MY BIG EYE

Owls cannot see in total darkness like you would find inside a windowless room or deep inside a cave. No animal has this superpower, because eyes need at least a glimmer of light in order to function. But owls do have incredible night vision.

Picture a mouse crouched in a long, dark hallway lit only by a single candle standing 390 yards (357 meters) away. That's all the illumination a barred owl, long-eared owl, great horned owl or barn owl perched 6 feet (1.8 meters) above the floor would need to spot that mouse and catch it. Those four species are among the most nocturnal owls in North America, and they can hunt in the faintest light. Other owls would need the candle to be a little closer to the mouse.

One reason owls see so well in the dark is that they have very big eyes for the size of their bodies. A full-grown great gray owl stands about 24 inches (61 centimeters) tall, but it has bigger eyeballs than most adult humans. Large eyes provide room for large pupils. The pupil is the opening in the center of the eye that lets in light. We see it as a black circle that expands in dim light and contracts in bright light. The bigger the pupil, the more light that enters the eye. The light projects images onto the *retina* at the back of the eye. The more light that enters the pupil, the brighter, bigger and sharper the images projected onto the retina.

Having big pupils is great when an owl is flying through the dark forest at night. But what happens if it suddenly veers into a bright moonlit clearing? When you walk out of a dark building onto a sunny street, you squint for a few minutes while your pupils shrink to let in less light. When you move from a bright space to a dark one, your eyes slowly adjust by enlarging the pupils. Owls don't have to wait. The size of their pupils changes almost instantly when the light level changes.

BLACK AND WHITE FOR THE NIGHT

Owls live in the same world we live in, but they see it differently. All animals have two types of cells that respond to light in their retinas: cones and rods. Cones are used for seeing fine details and color, and they need bright light to work properly. Rods work well in dim light, capturing rough shapes and movements in black, white and gray. Humans and most birds have more cones than rods in their retinas. We enjoy colorful daytime viewing but fumble around in the dark. Owls have far more rods than cones. That gives them the keen night sight they need to survive but very poor color vision.

An owl blinks the same way we do—by lowering its upper eyelids. But for sleeping, it raises the bottom eyelid to meet the top one. Each eye also has a thin, see-through inner eyelid, called a *nictitating membrane*. It cleans, moistens and protects the surface of the eyeball.

CARLOS CARRENO/GETTY IMAGES

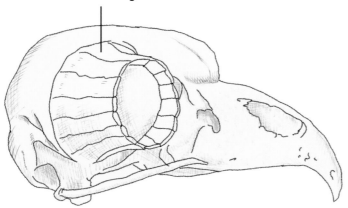

Sclerotic ring

An owl skull showing the bony collar that supports the eyeball. You can also see the true size of the bill. Normally we see only the curved tip of the bill because the rest is covered with feathers.

BUILT-IN BINOCULARS

Owl eyeballs aren't really balls. They are actually tube-shaped, like the two halves of a pair of binoculars. Like high-powered binoculars, they give owls outstanding long-distance vision. For example, a northern hawk owl can spot a tiny vole scampering across the ground almost half a mile (805 meters) away.

One downside of having tubular eyes is that they aren't good for focusing close up. Big owls have the hardest time focusing on close objects. For a snowy owl, anything that is less than 5.5 feet (1.7 meters) from its eyes will be blurry. Small to medium-sized owls can get to within about 10 inches (25 centimeters) of an object before they lose the ability to focus on it.

Another disadvantage is that owls can't roll their eyes from side to side or up and down like we can. Their long, tubular eyes stick out so far from the skull that they need extra support. A bony collar around each eye provides that support but also keeps the eye fixed in place. If an owl wants to look at something off to one side, it has to turn its whole head.

Owls make up for not being able to roll their eyes by having super-bendable necks. Even the most flexible human can swivel their head only a quarter turn to the left or right from center front. (Try it and see how you do.) But an owl can rotate its head more than halfway around its body to look directly behind its back. It can also tilt its head to turn its face nearly upside down. These talents come from having twice as many neck bones as we have.

A short-eared owl demonstrates the amazing owl trick of turning its head upside down. This position gives it a sharper view of anything that is above its head.

ZENO SWIJTINK/SHUTTERSTOCK.COM

WHO'S WHOO

Burrowing Owl

These small owls have round bodies and long, skinny legs. They live in dry short-grass habitats, usually in groups known as *colonies*. They do most of their hunting around dusk and dawn. During the breeding season they often spend time outside their burrows during the day. Burrowing owls are found from southern Canada to the tip of South America and in the West Indies. Their range includes southern parts of the Canadian prairies, much of the western United States and most of Florida. Most burrowing owls that breed in southern Canada and the northern United States are migratory.

BOBBLEHEADS

Owls have the most forward-facing eyes and the best three-dimensional vision of all birds. That gives them a great advantage when they are hunting because they can tell exactly how close their victims are as they pounce or swoop down on them. But owls get the 3-D effect only when they look straight ahead. If an owl is perched or standing and wants to pinpoint the position of something that isn't directly in front of its eyes, it has to change its point of view. It does this by moving its head up and down, backward and forward, or side to side.

Burrowing owls are famous for this behavior. They often stand just outside their burrows during the day, bobbing their heads as they survey their surroundings and watch for insects to eat. Some people call them howdy birds because they look like they are nodding hello.

Five young burrowing owls and a parent stand at their burrow entrance in South Dakota. Their home was made by prairie-dog neighbors like the ones in the background. When prairie dogs aren't using a burrow, burrowing owls borrow it.

HEAR, HEAR

Even with their specialized eyes, there are limits to how well owls can see at night. But they can always use their ears, no matter how dark it is. All owls have excellent hearing and can pick up many sounds that are too quiet for humans to detect.

The most nocturnal owls have the most sensitive ears. The faintest sounds of a scurrying mouse are enough to guide a barn owl or northern saw-whet owl straight to its invisible target. One reason owls hear so well is that their brains are packed with nerve cells that handle sound signals. They also have very big ear holes and inner ears.

Birds don't have ear flaps that stick out and funnel sounds into their ears, like we do. But owls get the same kind of boost from their *facial disk*. That's the flattish circle of feathers that rings an owl's face and looks a bit like a plate or shallow bowl. At the back of the facial disk is a dense ruff of stiff feathers that curves behind the ears and directs sounds toward the ear holes. The feathers in front of the ears are softer and looser. They create a screen that lets sound waves through to the ears but keeps bugs and dirt out.

Some owls, such as the great gray owl and barred owl, have a very clearly outlined facial disk. With others, such as the northern pygmy-owl, the edges blend into the rest of the head feathers. The facial disks of most North American owl species vary in shape from perfectly round to oval. The barn owl's heart-shaped face sets it apart from all the others.

A short-eared owl (top) and a barn owl (bottom).

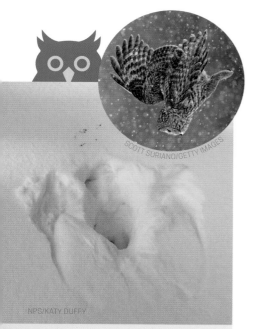

SCOTT SURIANO/GETTY IMAGES

NPS/KATY DUFFY

In winter great gray owls use their hearing to detect rodents hidden in snow tunnels up to 18 inches (46 centimeters) below the surface. Then they plunge into the snow to grab them. A great gray owl can punch through a crust that's thick enough to support a 175-pound (80-kilogram) person.

LOPSIDED LISTENING

When you hear a sound, you can tell which direction it's coming from because your brain automatically compares tiny differences in the sound waves that enter each of your ears. When the sound comes from the left, the sound waves are slightly stronger on that side and reach your left ear a moment sooner than they do your right ear. If you turn your head until the sound is equal on both sides, you end up facing the source of the sound.

This all happens because your ears are identical and evenly placed at the same level on either side of your head. Most owls also have matching ears, but at least 42 species don't. Having unevenly placed ears gives those owls a huge advantage when zeroing in on prey.

Owls that don't have matching ears generally have one ear hole that is higher than the other. Sound waves coming from below the owl's head reach the lower ear first. Many of these owls also have ear openings that are different sizes or shapes. And some have ear canals that tilt in different directions. All of these lopsided arrangements help owls get a quicker and more accurate fix on where sounds are coming from.

WHO'S WHOO

VISHAL SUBRAMANYAN

Great Gray Owl

Great gray owls live up to their name in color and size. They have a wingspan of up to 5 feet (1.5 meters) and fly with slow, deep wingbeats. Despite their long wings, they easily weave between tree trunks in dense forests. Great gray owls are found across northern regions of the world. In North America they live in the *boreal forest* from Alaska to Quebec and in western mountain forests. They are mainly nocturnal but often hunt by day during the nesting season and in winter.

DON'T BE FOOLED

When you look at certain owls, you might think you see ears. Even their names—like long-eared owl and short-eared owl—can fool you. But those things poking up from their heads are just feathers and have nothing to do with hearing. Biologists call them *ear tufts*.

About a quarter of the world's owl species have ear tufts. They help owls disguise themselves while roosting in trees or shrubs during the day. When an owl closes its eyes and erects its ear tufts, you can easily mistake it for a broken branch stub. Owls also seem to use their ear tufts for communicating with one another. They often raise or flatten them when interacting with mates or rivals.

Owlers find ear tufts helpful for identifying owls. Only two kinds of large owls with obvious ear tufts live in Canada and the United States—the long-eared owl and the great horned owl. Short-eared owls have short ear tufts and rarely raise them. Snowy owls have tiny ear tufts that are almost never visible. The small North American owls with the most noticeable ear tufts are screech-owls. Flammulated owls have short ear tufts and usually hold them flat, which makes their heads look square.

Western screech-owls and many other owls with ear tufts stretch up tall and raise their tufts high if they are startled while roosting. This posture may improve their camouflage by making them look more like the surrounding bark and branches.
©JARED HOBBS

WHO'S WHOO

VISHAL SUBRAMANYAN

Great Horned Owl

The range of this very adaptable owl covers most of Canada and the United States, much of Mexico and parts of Central and South America. Of all North American owls, great horned owls eat the greatest variety of prey—everything from grass-hoppers to great blue herons. They also use the widest variety of nest sites. One of the oddest ever found was a flowerpot on the balcony of a third-floor city apartment. Great horned owls are easily identified by their large size, prominent ear tufts and big yellow eyes.

Like all birds, owls regularly drop old, worn feathers, like this wing feather from a great horned owl, and replace them with new ones. Great horned owls replace only a few wing feathers each year, usually in summer or early fall.
FRANCES BACKHOUSE

FLYING IN SILENCE

Many of the night creatures that owls hunt have keen hearing. But most owls are stealthy fliers and can sneak up on their prey without being heard. The secret to their hushed flight is the design of their wing feathers, which have three unique features:

- ▶ Stiff bristles along the front edge of the feathers soften the sound of the wings cutting through the air.

- ▶ A soft fringe along the back edge of the feathers muffles the swoosh of air flowing off the wings.

- ▶ A velvety fuzz on the top surface of the feathers absorbs sounds.

If you find an owl feather on the ground, gently stroke the edges and top to feel these mufflers. You can also use the United States Fish and Wildlife Service's online feather identification tool to discover what species it came from.

Nocturnal owls are the quietest fliers. A quiet approach doesn't matter so much for owls that hunt in daylight or twilight, when their prey may see them. Silence is also less important for owls that eat mainly animals that can't hear them coming, like fish and most insects.

OWL FUEL

If you hate vegetables, you might enjoy being an owl because owls eat only animals. They mostly dine on mammals, birds and insects. But almost anything that scampers, crawls, swims or flies—and is a catchable size— ends up on the menu for some kind of owl. That includes bats, earthworms, snails, centipedes, scorpions, fish, frogs, tadpoles, crayfish, leeches, snakes and baby alligators. Some big owls also prey on smaller owls.

The main insect-eating owls in North America are the burrowing owl, elf owl, flammulated owl and ferruginous pygmy-owl. Their most common insect prey are grasshoppers, crickets, moths, beetles and cockroaches. During the colder months, when insects are scarce, they rely on other kinds of small prey. Lizards are a winter favorite of ferruginous pygmy-owls.

Great horned owls are the least fussy eaters of all North American owls. They hunt whatever is handy. Many other species have more specialized tastes. For example, snowy owls love lemmings. When these small Arctic mammals are plentiful during summer, snowy owls hunt almost nothing else, eating three to five of them a day. They only turn to other prey when lemmings aren't available.

A burrowing owl (top) munches on an insect. A ferruginous pygmy-owl (bottom) gets ready to devour a lizard.
(TOP) MARTHA MARKS/SHUTTERSTOCK.COM; (BOTTOM) DANITA DELIMONT/SHUTTERSTOCK.COM

A great horned owl with a freshly killed ground squirrel. When killing their prey, these powerful owls can clamp their talons so tight that it takes 29 pounds (13 kilograms) of force to open them.

The feet of most birds have three toes pointing forward and one pointing backward. An owl's foot has two toes that point forward, one that points backward and one that can point in either direction. Those movable toes help owls grasp prey. They also provide a strong grip for perching.

MOUSE POPSICLES

Owls usually polish off their prey right away, but sometimes they store uneaten portions or the whole thing. In some cases that's because they have too much to eat all at once. In others they are stocking up for the future, when hunting conditions might not be so good.

Storing food is a common survival technique for owls that live in places with harsh winter weather. But mouse popsicles are hard to eat. Boreal owls, northern saw-whet owls and others solve this problem by perching with their frozen meal tucked under their breast feathers, thawing it with their own body heat!

DEADLY WEAPONS

Owls catch prey mostly with their feet. As they approach their target, they spread the toes on each foot wide—two facing forward and two facing backward—to create as big a span as possible. The long claw at the end of each toe extends their reach. The moment an owl's feet strike its target, the toes lock into place like a clenched fist. This crushing grip and the sharp talons piercing the animal's body often deliver instant death. If not, the owl completes the kill with skull-crushing or backbone-cracking bites.

When a great horned owl's toes and talons are fully extended, each foot covers a rectangle measuring about 8 by 4 inches (20 by 10 centimeters). A tight squeeze from those huge feet can break the spine of an animal bigger than the owl itself. The northern pygmy-owl's much smaller weapons are just as deadly. Extra-long toes and talons help these owls tackle rodents and birds that weigh up to twice as much as they do.

An owl's beak is not well designed for catching prey because it curves downward instead of sticking straight out. But it's great for butchering and eating. And elf owls and screech-owls occasionally use their beaks to snap up flying insects.

GULP

By human standards owls have terrible table manners. They usually eat small prey, like mice, in one bite. No chewing. They just gulp down the whole animal headfirst. Their beaks seem so small that it's hard to believe how wide their mouths open. But when you look at an owl, you're seeing just the tip of its beak. The rest is hidden by feathers.

A northern hawk owl dines on a deer mouse. These owls usually swallow small prey whole. If they decide an animal is too big for one mouthful, they always start by removing and eating the head.
SHERI MINARDI PHOTOGRAPHY

Turning large animals into bite-sized portions takes a little longer. An owl uses the sharp edges of its beak to slice through flesh and bone, and the pointy hook to rip and tear. Its beak also functions like tweezers for removing feathers, insect wings, scorpion stingers and other bits the bird doesn't want to swallow. Whether it is eating its prey whole or in pieces, the owl often stuffs food into its mouth with one foot. If something is too big for easy swallowing, the bird jerks its head forward and back to wiggle it down. But owls aren't complete slobs. After a messy meal, they wipe their beaks and faces, usually on a branch or tree trunk. Snowy owls often use snow for their cleanup.

PUKE IT UP

Eating this way is efficient. But along with the good stuff, owls also scarf down lots of hard body parts, including bones, fur, feathers, claws, teeth, beaks, scales and insect heads, legs and wing cases. These scraps are too bulky and jagged to pass safely all the way through the gut. So the owl's digestive system sends them back the way they came.

After an owl swallows food its first stop is an area called the *gizzard*. There the digestible stuff is liquefied and sent on through the gut. Everything else remains in the gizzard for many hours and gets compacted into an oval **pellet**. Then the owl pukes it back up.

Owls usually produce one pellet a day. It may contain the remains of a single big animal or a number of small animals. Pellet size depends on the size of the owl. Pygmy-owl pellets are about an inch (2.5 centimeters) long. Pellets from great horned owls can be as long as 4 inches (10 centimeters). Not surprisingly, an owl can't eat anything else while it has this big lump sitting in its gizzard.

No one really knows how owls feel when they are ejecting a pellet, but it doesn't look like fun. The process often begins with the owl closing its eyes and scrunching up its facial disk, as if it's uncomfortable. Then it starts jerking and shaking its head, stretching its neck and opening and closing its beak. When the pellet finally reaches the mouth, the owl leans forward and lets it drop.

A great horned owl ejects a pellet. Other raptors and some other birds, including gulls, herons and crows, also produce pellets. But owl pellets are the most packed with bones and other undigested body parts.
VISHAL SUBRAMANYAN

WHO'S WHOO

©JARED HOBBS

Screech-Owls

North America has three screech-owl species. Eastern screech-owls live in the eastern half of the United States, plus parts of southern Canada and northeastern Mexico. Western screech-owls live along the west coast of Alaska and British Columbia, throughout the western United States and in much of Mexico. Whiskered screech-owls are found from southern Arizona and New Mexico to Central America. All three species are small and mainly nocturnal. They favor woodland and forest habitats and usually nest in tree holes. Eastern and western screech-owls readily use **nest boxes**. Whiskered screech-owls rarely do.

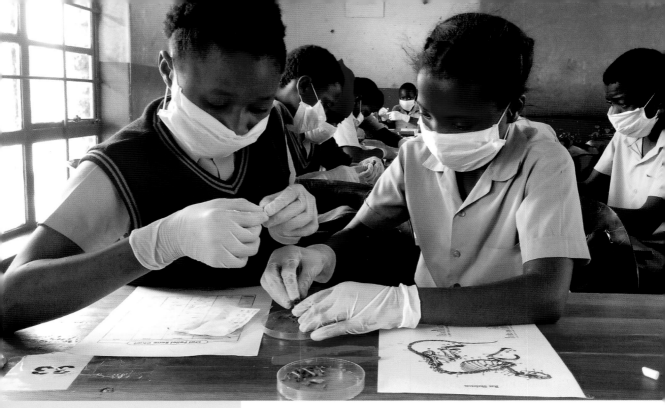

Students at a school in South Africa dissect barn owl pellets in science class. They are using a diagram of a rodent skeleton and a bone-sorting chart to discover what the owl ate.
OWLPROJECT.ORG

OWLPROJECT.ORG

PICKING APART PELLETS

Pellets are formed while owls sleep or rest. Owls usually get rid of them soon after they wake up and before they fly from their roost. Some owls use a favorite roost over and over. So if you find a pellet on the ground—or a pile of pellets—look up. You might see a sleepy owl.

Biologists often collect and dissect pellets because they're full of clues about what owls eat. As they separate out the different bits, they try to identify the prey they came from. Are the bones hollow? Then they're from a bird. Is there fur? Then a mammal was on the menu. Close examination of feathers, beaks, teeth, skulls and other bones may reveal exactly what kind of bird or mammal. Experts can even identify different kinds of insects by looking at their body parts.

A TREASURE HUNT

If you would like to do your own owl-diet investigation, you can buy sterilized pellets from companies that sell nature-study supplies or places like the International Owl Center. You can also collect pellets and sterilize them by soaking them in a 10 percent bleach solution for a few hours or wrapping them in foil and baking them for 40 minutes at 325°F (163°C). Just make sure you get permission before you pop them in the oven. Pellets have no odor at room temperature, but they get smelly when they are heated.

When handling unsterilized owl pellets, always wear disposable gloves and keep your hands away from your face. To be on the safe side, you should take the same precautions with sterilized pellets. In either case, cover your work surface with newspaper or paper towels before you start dissecting, and clean up well after you're done. That includes thoroughly washing your hands with soap and water.

How can you tell owl pellets from mammal droppings? Owl pellets, like these two examples, are usually rounded on both ends and often contain bones. They also aren't stinky. Mammal poop has more pointed ends and rarely contains bones. Remember this rule: "If you can smell it, it isn't a pellet."
NPS/JEFF FOOTT

You don't need any special tools to pick apart a pellet. Toothpicks, popsicle sticks, tweezers and fingers work fine. You can soak the pellet in warm water to soften it before you start dissecting. Or leave it dry and gently pry it apart.

Every pellet is like a treasure chest. You never know what you might find inside.

NPS/JEFF FOOTT

> "Owls are an eco-friendly form of pest control."
> —Adivhaho Mokakatleng

Marlboro Gardens Secondary School students stand proudly beside a barn-owl box that will be put up in their schoolyard. The man in the T-shirt works for owlproject.org. He brought the box and some owls who needed a new home.

OWLPROJECT.ORG

OWL ALLIES

Owls at School

Barn Owl (Tyto alba) Food Chain

MOTLATSI ZULU

OWLPROJECT.ORG

Marlboro Gardens Secondary School in Johannesburg, South Africa, has some unusual tenants. They live just outside the classroom windows but only come out at night when everyone has gone home. These tenants are barn owls, brought to the school by an organization called owlproject.org. The organization also put up the wooden boxes the owls use for roosting and nesting.

Adivhaho Mokakatleng was in sixth grade at Marlboro Gardens when he saw his first barn owl. An owlproject.org staff member was delivering three new owls to the school. Before placing them in their release box, he showed them to the students. Adivhaho was surprised at how big they were, even though they weren't full-grown. The owls needed to get used to their new home, so they were kept inside the release box for three weeks and fed by the students. Once they were allowed to come and go freely, they could find lots of prey right on the school grounds.

These young owls were moved from a nearby neighborhood because people there were afraid of them. That fear is common in South Africa, where owls are traditionally associated with witchcraft. But Marlboro Gardens students are learning that owls are actually helpful, not evil.

"It is good to have owls at our school because they kill rodents," says Adivhaho.

Marlboro Gardens is in an area that has rodent infestations. The students may never see the owls hunting, but they can prove that the birds have a big impact on reducing the number of rats and mice around the school. All they have to do is examine the pellets the owls spit up after processing their meals.

Owlproject.org has put owl boxes in many places around Johannesburg. It collects pellets from these sites for its Junior Scientist program. Students who take part in the program dissect the pellets and use skeleton diagrams and identification keys to figure out what the owls ate.

Adivhaho's teacher, Mrs. Zulu, says many students used to be scared of owls. Now that they share their schoolyard with these birds, they understand them better and appreciate their value.

A burrowing owl in Florida calls while standing in its burrow entrance. Burrowing owls mainly call when they are close to their nest burrow.

3

Owl Life

HOOTS, TOOTS, TRILLS AND MORE

Owls rely heavily on their voices for communicating with one another. Eavesdropping on their conversations also helps curious humans figure out who they are and what they're up to. No matter how dark it is, owls can be identified by the special calls they use to advertise their territories to rivals and potential mates. Many owl species hoot, but each in its own way. For example, the long-eared owl's hoot sounds like someone blowing across the top of a glass bottle. The great horned owl's sounds like a distant foghorn.

Other owl calls include toots, trills, whistles and coos. Barn owls give long, eerie shrieks. Eastern screech-owls whinny like horses, with high-pitched voices. And the Australian barking owl's *woof-woof* sounds so much like a dog that real dogs sometimes bark back at them.

Two of the most commonly heard hooters in North America are the great horned owl and the barred owl. Great horned owls hoot with a steady rhythm as they deliver a series of three to six deep *whoo*s. The barred owl's main call has two parts, often repeated several times in a row. Each part usually starts with two or three low *hoo*s and ends with a loud *hoo-ooo*—as if the owl is asking, "Who cooks for you? Who cooks for you all?"

Harriet Tubman's knowledge of nature helped her lead dozens of enslaved people to freedom in the mid-1800s. She imitated the barred owl's call to tell the people she was guiding when they could safely come out of hiding at night and continue their dangerous journeys.

VOICES BIG AND SMALL

In general, the bigger the owl, the louder its voice. The booming hoots of male snowy owls can be heard across the Arctic **tundra** from several miles away. But not all big owls are loud. You have to be within half a mile (800 meters) of a great gray owl to hear its soft hoots. Flammulated owls are small owls with big voices. Their short, low-pitched hoots can carry just as far as a great gray owl's. But finding flammulated owls can be tricky because they often throw their voices, so their calls seem to come from farther away.

WHO'S WHOO

©JARED HOBBS

Flammulated Owl

Flammulated owls are North America's second-smallest owl and the continent's only small owl with dark-brown eyes. (The others have yellow eyes.) They nest in tree holes and eat almost nothing but insects, such as moths, beetles, crickets and grasshoppers. Flammulated owls are found in dry open forests in scattered locations from southern British Columbia to central Mexico. Those that breed in Canada and the United States spend their winters in Mexico and Central America.

OWL TALK FOR EVERY OCCASION

Some kinds of owls mate with the same partner every year for as long as they are both alive. Others stay together for only one breeding season. Whether they are reconnecting with their old mate or trying to attract a new one, they all use their voices when they are courting.

During the breeding season you might hear a male and female owl calling back and forth to each other. This is known as *duetting*. Barred-owl duets are a rowdy jumble of cackles, chortles, caws and hoots that often goes on for several minutes. Other species that perform duets include great horned owls and western screech-owls.

But there's more to owl talk than just claiming territories and getting together with mates. Alarm calls warn of danger and repel enemies. Contact calls keep family members connected when they can't see each other. Feeding calls are exchanged when males bring food to their mates or parents feed their young.

PHONY PUPPIES AND FAKE RATTLERS

Owls start using their voices almost as soon as they hatch and sometimes before. Their first calls are quiet peeps, squeaks or twitters. As they get older they turn up the volume, especially when they're hungry. Noisy demands for food can lead sharp-eared owlers to hidden nests. If you're out in the desert in the southwestern United States or northern Mexico and think you hear puppies yipping, look around for a saguaro cactus with a hole in it. Chances are, the yips are coming from a nest tucked full of young elf owls.

Predators can just as easily follow the sounds of hungry chicks, but owl parents are fierce guardians. Young burrowing owls also have a trick to ward off enemies such as badgers. When frightened they make a call that sounds just like the rattling tail of an annoyed rattlesnake. No smart badger that hears that buzz is going to risk nosing deep into a dark burrow to find out if it's the real thing. The fake rattle can fool humans too. Some people who hear it think burrowing owls share their homes with rattlesnakes. Research has proven that's not true.

An elf owl peers out of its nest hole in a saguaro cactus in Arizona. Its desert home can get very hot in the day and very cold at night. Nesting in an old woodpecker hole provides protection against extreme temperatures.
©JARED HOBBS

BODY LANGUAGE

Screams, screeches or angry scolding are often enough to drive off a predator or trespasser. But sometimes owls add emphasis with a threat display—ruffling up their body feathers, lowering their heads, crouching, drooping their wings and swaying from side to side. Some kinds of owls will also raise their wings and fan them out above and beside their heads. This body language aims to make the owl look bigger and scarier. Throw in some hissing and bill snapping, and it's pretty intimidating. If those actions don't get the message across, the owl's next step will be to attack.

Several owl species use distraction displays to deal with danger. They pretend to be injured to lure predators or people away from their nest or their young. Short-eared owls create these distractions by tumbling out of the sky and flapping around on the ground, crying pitifully. Whenever the predator gets close, the owl flies a short distance away and then repeats its very convincing act. Snowy owls are also masters of this art. One mother snowy owl led a biologist 2 miles (3.2 kilometers) across the tundra, flopping and flailing, squealing and squawking all the way.

Relaxed owls normally have their top eyelids slightly lowered. Wide-open round eyes indicate that these young great horned owls are on high alert. The body language of the one on the left says that it's seriously scared and anxious.

4LOOPS/GETTY IMAGES

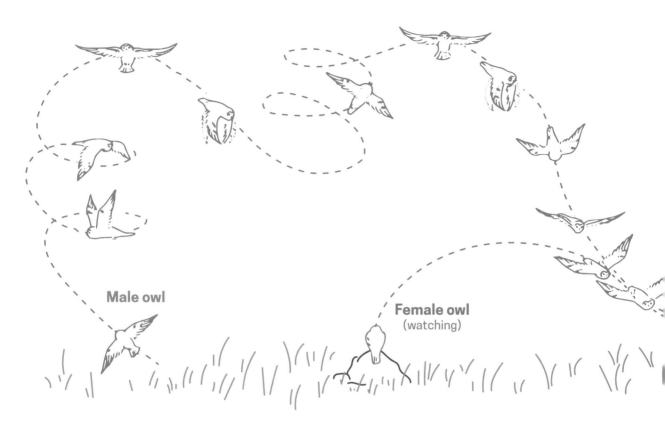

Male owl

Female owl
(watching)

A male short-eared owl's courtship sky dance follows an elaborate flight path. The female owl watches from the ground. Sometimes she will fly up and chase him as he swoops past her on the downward track.

ADAPTED FROM "BIRDS OF NORTH AMERICA," CORNELL LAB OF ORNITHOLOGY AND AMERICAN ORNITHOLOGICAL SOCIETY, 1992

MANY WAYS OF WOOING

Body language is also an important part of courtship for many owl species. Courtship displays can be as simple as a male popping in and out of a nest hole to encourage a female to check it out, or as showy as the short-eared owl's sky dance. Male short-eared owls dance from mid-February to late June, in the daytime and at night. Starting close to the ground, the performer flies in tight circles high into the air and then drops abruptly for a short distance while clapping his wings below his body. The wing claps sound like a person rapidly slapping their hands against their thighs. Then he spirals upward again, pauses at the top to toot out a short string of notes and dives back down with more wing clapping. The female he is trying to impress watches from the ground and cheers him on with an occasional *keeeyup*.

- ▶ Long-eared owls and northern hawk owls also engage in fancy flying and wing claps to woo mates.

- ▶ Great horned owls do their whole routine while perched on a tree branch, bowing, raising their tail and puffing out their bib of white neck feathers.

- ▶ Snowy owls have a complex act that starts in the air and ends on the ground with the male leaning so far forward that he's almost lying down.

HOMES ON HIGH

Once owls decide who to mate with, their next task is to prepare for nesting. Most species of owls don't build their own nests. Instead they move into empty homes made by other animals or claim other kinds of sites that suit their needs.

Large owls are generally platform nesters. The platform is often an old stick nest built by a hawk, eagle, heron, raven, crow or magpie. Other popular choices include a cliff ledge or the bowl-shaped top of a broken tree trunk. The best platform-nest sites are sheltered and hidden by branches or an overhanging shelf of rock.

Small and medium-sized owls tend to be cavity, or hole, nesters. They often take over abandoned woodpecker nests in trees and cactuses. Woodpeckers usually make a new nest hole every year, so there are lots of vacancies.

An eastern screech-owl pokes its head out of its nest hole in a palm tree. Eastern screech-owls that can't find an abandoned woodpecker hole or other natural nest site will use a wide variety of other options—even mailboxes!
CALV6304/DREAMSTIME.COM

And these hand-me-down homes have thick walls that provide excellent protection from weather and predators. Spotted owls and barred owls also like to nest in holes, but they are too big to squeeze into woodpecker cavities. Instead they look for spaces created by rot, such as the hollowed-out top of a broken tree trunk or a large knothole. Sometimes they have to make do with a platform nest.

Barn owls nest in all sorts of nooks and hollows, from holes in trees to spaces inside church steeples. They particularly like nesting in barns, because there is usually plenty of prey nearby. It's like living next to a grocery store.

NESTING DOWN LOW

Platform-nesting owls occasionally nest at ground level when they can't find a good elevated site. But snowy owls and short-eared owls always have to nest on the ground because they breed in areas with few or no trees. Female snowy owls on the tundra make nests called scrapes. First they scratch with their feet to clear away twigs and stones. Then they swivel their bodies against the ground to form a shallow depression. Female short-eared owls use their bodies the same way to shape tall grasses into a bowl. They line their nests with grass or downy feathers.

Burrowing owls are the only North American raptors (birds of prey) that nest underground. Those that live in Florida usually dig their own burrows. In the western United States and Canada, they almost always leave the hard labor to others, including ground squirrels, badgers, prairie dogs, marmots, skunks, armadillos, kangaroo rats and tortoises. If you see a western burrowing owl kicking soil out of a burrow, it's probably doing renovations or home maintenance, not new construction.

Burrowing owls have some odd decorating habits, which biologists are still trying to understand. When nesting, the owls often scatter pieces of dried mammal dung, such as cow patties, in and around their burrow entrance. The dung attracts dung beetles, which the owls eat, so their purpose might be to bring food to the family's doorstep—like pizza delivery where the pizza delivers itself. But sometimes burrowing owls also adorn their doorways with different kinds of debris, such as grass, bones, pebbles, shredded paper or bottle caps. These decorations may be like a "sold" sign announcing that the burrow is taken.

These fuzzy short-eared owl chicks are a day or two old. The other eggs will hatch within the next couple of days. The owlets will develop quickly and leave their nest when they are about two weeks old.
NATALIE FOBES/GETTY IMAGES

A great gray owl watches over her chicks. The hawks or ravens who built this stick nest have moved on. If this owl and her mate like the nest, they may use it again for several years.

JEFF FOOTT/GETTY IMAGES

OWL EGGS-CELLENCE

If someone gave you a freshly killed rat as a gift, you probably wouldn't be thrilled—unless you were an owl. Delivering dead prey is how a male owl tells a potential partner that he's serious about settling down and will be a good mate and father.

Owl eggs are big, and it takes a lot of energy to produce them, so females need to fatten up before they can start laying. To do that, they rely on their mates to bring them food instead of hunting for themselves. Some gain so much weight during this time that they have trouble flying. Female owls also need to take a long break after laying each egg. They always pause for at least one day and sometimes for two to three. Great horned owls occasionally lay their eggs a whole week apart.

Clutch size depends on the species and how well fed the mother is. For example, great horned owls usually lay only one or two eggs, but their record is five. Snowy owls lay up to 11 eggs when lemmings—their main prey—are plentiful, but just a few or none at all when lemmings are in short supply. For many other species, clutches of two to four eggs are common.

How long owls *incubate* their eggs also varies between species. Generally it's about a month. Most North American owls start incubating as soon as they have one egg. The first egg hatches first, and the others follow one by one at the same pace as they were produced. If the clutch is large, or the eggs were each laid a few days apart, the oldest *nestling* will be a week or two older than its youngest sibling.

A great horned owl sits on her nest in an April snowstorm with her nestlings tucked out of sight beneath her body. Mothers of this species often endure harsh weather during their month-long incubation period and when their chicks are very young.

DAVE ALEXANDER

TEAMWORK

Owl parents work as a team. Females incubate the eggs and care for the nestlings. Males feed and guard their families. Mother owls hardly leave the nest from the start of incubation until the chicks are a few weeks old. This can be tough on owls that live in cold regions or start nesting early in the year, such as great horned owls and great gray owls. They sit tight even when temperatures plunge below freezing or snow piles up around them.

Before a female owl begins laying eggs each year, she develops a built-in heating pad on her belly, called a brood patch. The brood patch loses its feathers and builds up extra blood vessels to carry warm blood to the bare skin. It also softens and swells so it can tuck in like a quilt around the eggs and, later, around the nestlings. The

Male owls of many species store extra prey in or near their nest during the breeding season. Barn owls often stockpile 30 to 50 dead rodents, but one extra enthusiastic dad stashed 189! Another exceptional provider was a great horned owl who stuffed 12 snowshoe hares into his nest.

male's work begins with hunting for two while the female incubates the eggs. A great gray owl must catch an extra three to five rodents each night for his mate. Male elf owls deliver insects to their partners every two to five minutes from dusk to dawn. Once the eggs hatch, owl fathers have to provide even more food.

New babies also mean more work for moms. For the first week or so, mothers supervise every meal and divvy up the food. They dice up prey such as mammals and birds into fleshy fragments and crush hard invertebrates. They also remove bones, fur, stingers and other indigestible parts.

Once nestlings are big enough to keep themselves warm, their mother starts hunting again. That means she can feed herself and help her mate feed their family.

A great gray owl feeds her 24-day-old chick with prey provided by her mate. Young great gray owls leave the nest at three to four weeks old. After that their father is the main caregiver until they can hunt for themselves.

JAMES HAGER/GETTY IMAGES

NESTLING LIFE

Owls emerge from their shells wet, blind and helpless. A newly hatched owl has a tiny body and a big head weighed down by an oversized bill. It can prop itself up on its stubby wings, but its legs are too weak to bear any weight. Its eyes will stay sealed shut for several days. The hatchling looks almost naked until its short downy feathers dry out and fluff up. Over the next week or two, its whitish fuzz is replaced by long, soft, light-brown or gray feathers. Flight feathers also start to sprout on its wings and tail.

Owlets of different species develop at different rates. Within 24 hours of hatching, they all start to crawl, open their bills to beg for food and feebly grasp the morsels their mothers offer them. Some are strong enough to hold their heads up and stand tall after just a week. Others take a little longer. Snowy owl chicks grow especially fast. At hatching they weigh about 1 to 2 ounces (28 to 57 grams). Three weeks later they tip the scales at over 1 pound (454 grams) and are ready to leave their nest. Short-eared owls head out when they're just two weeks old. Both of these species depart as soon as possible because they are easy targets for predators when they are in their nests on the ground. At the other end of the scale, great horned owls don't exit their nests until they are six weeks old. Barn owls wait even longer.

Leeza Chamberland cradles a couple of baby northern saw-whet owls. Her father has briefly taken them from their nest box to give them identification leg bands. Only people who have a government bird-banding permit are allowed to do this. Thirteen-year-old Leeza is an enthusiastic bird-bander trainee.

RICHARD CHAMBERLAND

LEAVING HOME

A young bird that has recently left its nest is called a *fledgling*. Fledglings of most owl species never go back to their nest once they leave for the first time. Many can't return because the nest becomes too crowded for a bunch of growing owls. Some stay away because they are safer out of the nest. Only two North American species—barn owls and burrowing owls—come and go from their nest as fledglings.

Barn owls make their first awkward flights when they are seven or eight weeks old. Their mother then moves out of the nest while the owlets stick around for several more weeks. Both parents keep bringing food to their offspring until they have honed their flying and hunting skills. Once the meal service ends, the youngsters leave for good.

Burrowing owls emerge from their nest burrow about two weeks after hatching but remain in residence until they are about two months old. At first they never stray more than a few feet from the entrance as they wait for food deliveries and practice running, hopping and flapping. Short training flights start a couple of weeks later. Finally they graduate to chasing insects. The nest burrow is always home base until they can fully fend for themselves.

A family of ferruginous pygmy-owls lines up on a branch shortly after leaving their nest. Fledglings of this species stick close together for about five weeks, often perching less than 11 yards (10 meters) apart.
NPS/PUBLIC DOMAIN

WHO'S WHOO

Northern Hawk Owl

Northern hawk owls live in the northern forests of Eurasia and North America. Winter **irruptions** periodically bring them into southwestern Canada and the northern United States. They are very nomadic, often changing their breeding locations as their food supply changes. Their long tails and short pointed wings give these medium-sized owls a hawklike appearance. They hunt from high perches and lean far forward when scanning for prey instead of sitting erect as other owls do. They usually nest in tree holes and occasionally in old stick nests made by other birds.

NPS/EMILY MESNER

A fledgling barred owl uses its sharp talons to haul itself up a tree. Young flightless owls often explore the world by climbing from branch to branch and are sometimes called *branchers*.
SCOTT SURIANO/GETTY IMAGES

FLIGHT PATH TO INDEPENDENCE

Most young owls have little or no flying ability when they say goodbye to their nest. Ground nesters can depart on foot. Hole nesters and platform nesters either clamber out onto a branch or flutter, jump or tumble to the ground or a nearby perch. If nestlings are too timid to make that first scary move, their parents coax them with encouraging calls or tempt them with food.

Being flightless doesn't stop fledglings from getting around. On the ground they walk, run and hop. Some are also experts at moving about in trees and bushes. They go up, down and sideways—climbing foot over foot, grabbing twigs and bark with their beaks and flapping their wings for balance.

Boreal owls and northern saw-whet owls are exceptions. They fly reasonably well as soon as they leave the nest. Elf owls can also fly right away but only weakly. Other small owls generally get airborne within a few days. Larger owls take longer.

SURVIVAL ODDS

It takes anywhere from a few weeks to a few months for young owls to become fully independent. During that time they still need their parents to feed, protect and teach them. Once they finally split up from their parents and siblings, they may remain close to where they were raised or travel some distance before settling. By the next breeding season they will be ready to start their own families—if they survive.

Many owls die before their first birthday, usually because they can't feed themselves well enough or aren't experienced enough to dodge predators. Starvation and predation are also the most common natural causes of death for adults. But an owl's survival odds improve greatly if it gets through its first year. Generally the larger the owl, the longer its potential life span. Tiny elf owls rarely live beyond four years in the wild. Some great horned owls reach their late twenties.

PACK YOUR BAGS

Many owls never move far from their adult home once they find it. But some make yearly journeys back and forth between their breeding grounds and their winter home to get the best weather and hunting opportunities

Leeza Chamberland holds two young great horned owls that her father is about to band. Leeza and her father will also record each bird's age and size. He climbed up to their nest to collect the owlets and will put them back as soon as he and Leeza are done.
RICHARD CHAMBERLAND

in each season. This regular pattern of movement is called *migration*. In some cases, not all members of a species migrate. For example, burrowing owls that nest in Canada and the northern United States are migratory, but their relatives in warmer places, such as Florida and southern California, stay put year-round.

The unique identification number on this burrowing owl's leg band helps researchers track its travels. On this cool spring day, it has just returned to its breeding grounds in southern British Columbia after spending the winter somewhere in Mexico.
BURROWING OWL CONSERVATION SOCIETY OF BC

A snowy owl sits on a New Jersey beach in the winter. This owl's summer home is far to the north, in the Arctic.
VICKI JAURON, BABYLON AND BEYOND PHOTOGRAPHY/GETTY IMAGES

Depending on where they nest, long-eared owls may be either migrants or nomads. Both groups often travel far to reach wintering grounds. Two of their longest recorded journeys were from Saskatchewan to southern Mexico, a trip of about 2,400 miles (3,862 kilometers), and from the northern United States to central Mexico, a distance of more than 1,800 miles (2,897 kilometers).

WANDERERS

Owls whose long-distance travel is less predictable are called *wanderers* or *nomads*. They don't always follow the same route or return to the same breeding or wintering areas the way migrants do. Some years they may not go anywhere at all.

North America's nomadic owls include great gray owls, northern hawk owls, boreal owls and snowy owls. Their wandering ways have a lot to do with their very changeable food supply. All of them are specialist hunters of small mammals such as lemmings, voles and snowshoe hares, whose numbers rise and fall dramatically from year to year.

Every few winters large numbers of nomadic owls appear in places far from where they are normally seen. This kind of mass movement is known as an irruption. One year it could be a blizzard of snowy owls in the northeastern states. Another year it's thousands of great gray owls ghosting through forests south of the Great Lakes.

These spectacles draw crowds. Not only are there lots of owls, but they are often easy to spot because they are out in the open or perched in leafless trees. Owlers flock to see the rare visitors. Biologists grab the chance to learn more about owl life. And even people who were never interested in owls before get drawn in by the excitement.

A snowy owl skims above the Arctic tundra near Utqiaġvik, AK—the town that used to be named Barrow. In the Iñupiaq language, utqiaġvik means "the place where we hunt snowy owls."
RICCARDO SAVI/GETTY IMAGES

OWL ALLIES

Counting Owls in the Night

It's late at night, and the Barney family is standing by their car on a dark back road in New Brunswick. Suddenly two barred owls swoop out of the woods, land in a big tree next to the car and start hooting. "They were duetting for a long time," Jaden Barney says, remembering the scene. "It was pretty cool."

Every spring more than 1,000 volunteers fan out across Canada to listen to—and count—nocturnal owls for a survey run by Birds Canada. The information they gather supports owl conservation. Jaden's family started participating when he was 12 and his sister, Zoe, was seven.

Every survey team is assigned a route and chooses one night during the survey period to do their count. Most routes are about 10 miles (16 kilometers) long, with a stopping point every mile (1.6 kilometers). At each stop the surveyors get out and play a recording of owl calls. It starts with two minutes of silence, giving the team a chance to detect any owls that are already calling. There are short silences between calls so they can listen for responses. Whenever they hear an owl, they write down the time, location and species. Jaden, Zoe and their parents mostly hear barred owls, great horned owls and northern saw-whet owls.

By the time the Barneys reach the end of their route, it's usually around midnight. "You get really tired close to the end," Jaden admits. But as a keen birder, he doesn't mind. "It's definitely fun, because you never really know when one's going to start calling." Or, better yet, show itself—like that unforgettable pair of barred owls.

LIZA BARNEY

> **"In the dark you can't see them coming. Sometimes they just come out of nowhere."**
> —Jaden Barney

A flock of kids wearing owl masks and
T-shirts poses on a forest trail.
REBECCA EMERY/GETTY IMAGES

Giving a Hoot

OWLS UNDER PRESSURE

As we discovered earlier, owls all around the world are under pressure. The number one threat is habitat loss. Eating poisoned rodents and colliding with cars and planes are also major problems that affect many species.

Fortunately, owls have plenty of supporters who are helping them. Some do research to get a better understanding of what owls need to succeed. Some work on conservation projects. Some contribute through individual actions. Whatever your age, experience and skills, there are ways you can get involved and show you give a hoot about owls. Let's get started!

A burrowing owl stands beside an artificial burrow in Cibola National Wildlife Refuge near the Arizona–California border. This refuge is one of many places in North America where people are working to bring back burrowing owls.

NCTC IMAGE LIBRARY/PUBLIC DOMAIN

TAKE ACTION: Help catalog photos of burrowing owls. The Wildwatch Burrowing Owl project accepts volunteers of all ages.

NOTHING SAYS "WELCOME" LIKE FAKE OWL POOP

Burrowing owls have disappeared or are in danger of disappearing from many areas where they once lived in Canada and the United States. Various recovery programs are trying to bring them back or help them hang on. In southern California, the San Diego Zoo Wildlife Alliance leads one of these programs. It includes relocating burrowing owls whose habitat is threatened by the construction of houses and businesses. But they can't simply catch the owls and drop them off at a new address. They have to ensure there are suitable owl homes there.

Southern California burrowing owls normally nest in holes dug by ground squirrels. But some relocation sites lack these natural burrows because all the ground squirrels have been killed off by people who see them as pests. To make up for the missing housing, the recovery-program biologists build artificial burrows. They also encourage ground squirrels to return and expand the owl neighborhood.

The biologists do all they can to entice the owls to settle in and discourage them from flying back to familiar territory. Before moving day, they squirt white paint around each artificial-burrow entrance. This fake owl poop is like a welcome mat that makes it look like other owls have already lived in the home and approved it. The newcomers are also greeted with recorded burrowing owl calls. The soundtrack creates a friendly vibe because burrowing owls like to live in groups.

Motion-activated cameras are set up outside some of the burrows to gather information about the owls. Each camera takes tens of thousands of photos during a single breeding season, and every one must be cataloged. That means recording such information as the number of owls in the photo, whether they are adults or juveniles and what they are doing. Volunteer **citizen scientists** do much of the cataloging. They work online through the Wildwatch Burrowing Owl website.

SOLAR-POWERED SNOWY-OWL STUDIES

The winter behavior of snowy owls is a puzzle. A few incredibly hardy individuals remain in the Arctic year-round. The rest scatter southward in the fall. Down south, snowy owls seek out flat, treeless places similar to their northern habitat, such as beaches, farm fields and airport lands. But owls that hang around airports run a high risk of being struck by planes or killed to prevent them from causing plane crashes. Other unfamiliar southern dangers include being hit by cars or electrocuted by power lines.

Some years snowy owls travel farther and in greater numbers than usual. In the winter of 2013–14, they showed up in odd places all across the continent—from Vancouver Island to Newfoundland, and as far south as Mississippi and Florida. As their numbers surged in the northeastern states, owl lovers there joined forces to keep the visitors safe and learn more about them. Project SNOWstorm, as they called it, is now one of the world's largest snowy-owl research programs.

Every winter, SNOWstorm team members capture snowy owls and move them away from airports to keep them out of danger. These owls, along with ones caught in other locations, are sent off wearing small solar-powered transmitter backpacks, attached with a harness that loops

Snowy owls that winter in the Arctic sometimes move north onto the frozen ocean and hunt for ducks in open water gaps between ice sheets. Down south, some follow the same strategy out on the frozen Great Lakes. They prey on waterbirds they find in areas where the ice has cracked open.

TAKE ACTION: Go on the Project SNOWstorm website to track the movements of their backpack-carrying owls and explore interactive maps of their journeys.

A citizen scientist holds a snowy owl nicknamed Newton, who is wearing a transmitter backpack. Newton's nearly pure-white plumage means he's at least five years old. He was captured in January 2023 in southern Ontario. You can track his movements on the Project SNOWstorm website.
CHARLOTTE ENGLAND

over the wings. The transmitter records the owl's location, altitude and flight speed at least once an hour and sends the data to the project's computers. The team may never see the birds again, but they can track their travels for years to come.

Information from the transmitters helps the researchers learn how to move snowy owls away from risky locations in the safest and most effective way. It also allows them to study the owls from afar when they return to remote parts of the Arctic.

NETTING SECRETIVE SAW-WHETS

Northern saw-whet owls move almost invisibly between their breeding and wintering grounds. These small forest owls travel only at night, fly silently and stay well hidden when resting. The only reliable way to study migrating saw-whets is to go out in the woods in the dark and intercept them. That's Project Owlnet's mission.

Project Owlnet involves hundreds of independent researchers and citizen scientists. They study owls at more than 125 sites across North America and share their findings.

A night of Owlnet research starts with setting up a line of mist nets. These look like oversized volleyball nets but are made from fine mesh that holds birds without harming them. Shortly after dusk the researchers switch on a recording of the saw-whet owl's territorial call that plays on an endless loop. When curious owls come to investigate the steady *toot-toot-toot*, they fly into the almost-invisible nets.

Net monitors check frequently for new arrivals, gently untangle the captives and carry them to a sheltered

WHO'S WHOO

Northern Saw-Whet Owl

Northern saw-whet owls breed in forests and woodlands across southern Canada and the northern United States, and from southern Alaska to southern Mexico. Many move south in winter. Irruptions are common in the eastern United States. These small, stubby owls are almost entirely nocturnal and are more often heard than seen. During the day they roost in dense vegetation. Their natural nest sites are abandoned woodpecker holes, but they will readily use artificial nest boxes.

TOM WALKER/GETTY IMAGES

processing area. They tuck the owls into cloth bags to keep them safe, dry and warm while in transit. At the processing area, the researchers record the owl's weight, age, sex and condition. They also give it an aluminum leg band with a unique identification number. If the owl already has one of these tiny ID bracelets, they write down the number. Once processed, the owl is carried back out into the dark and released.

Project Owlnet has answered many questions about northern saw-whet owls but is still working on others. The more we learn, the better we can care for this secretive species.

TAKE ACTION: Help biologists collect valuable information about migration and other bird behavior by joining eBird— a global online community of birders—and sharing your sightings. One section of the eBird website provides resources for young birders.

A young citizen scientist with a northern saw-whet owl at a migration research station. Sometimes the researchers wait hours before any owls show up. But at the peak of fall migration, the busiest stations may catch more than 100 in a night.
ANDREW JAKES

A pair of California State Park employees share their excitement about the Poo-Poo screen they have just put in place on an outhouse ventilation pipe to keep wildlife out of this dangerous space.
CALIFORNIA STATE PARKS/COURTESY OF TETON RAPTOR CENTER

TAKE ACTION: Raise money to sponsor Poo-Poo screens. If you see an outhouse in a park or recreation site that needs a screen, talk to the people in charge about adding one.

KEEPING OWLS OUT OF OUTHOUSES

Nobody likes to linger in an outhouse, especially a stinky one. So imagine how awful it would be to get trapped in that disgusting hole below the toilet seat! Outhouses that don't use water for flushing are common in camp-grounds, at trailheads and in other outdoor locations. They may be vault toilets with a holding tank that gets pumped out when it's full, or pit toilets where the waste is just left to rot. They often have a wide pipe running from the tank or pit up through the roof to let out heat and smells. Every year countless birds tumble down those pipes.

Most of the victims are birds that nest and roost in holes, including many owls. To them the open end of a pipe probably looks like a nook in the top of a broken tree trunk. Before they realize their mistake, they're in deep trouble, with little chance of escape or rescue.

The Poo-Poo Project—short for the Port-O-Potty Owl Project—is working to put an end to these accidents. Staff at the Teton Raptor Center in Wyoming started the project after seeing some icky photos of a boreal owl stuck at the bottom of a vault toilet. That owl was pulled out, cleaned off and released unharmed. Most birds that end up in this predicament aren't so lucky.

The Poo-Poo Project has developed a screen for covering outhouse pipes that is strong, inexpensive and easy to attach. Air can flow out, but wildlife can't get in. Since 2013 more than 18,000 Poo-Poo screens have been installed throughout North America.

When he was 16 years old, Bjorn Tolman installed 21 of those screens in Antelope Island State Park near his home in Utah. For Bjorn it was a satisfying Eagle Scout service project. For the island's barn owls and other birds that nest and roost in holes, it was a lifesaving gift.

POISONING PREVENTION

Poison might seem like a simple way to solve rodent problems on farms, around homes and in food-focused businesses like restaurants and grocery stores. But it actually makes things worse in the long term because it kills off their natural predators, such as owls. People who put out

Bjorn Tolman stands on top of an outhouse in Antelope Island State Park as he attaches a Poo-Poo screen to the ventilation pipe.
TETON RAPTOR CENTER

Barn owls are rodent-control champions. A typical barn-owl family polishes off 1,000 to 3,000 rodents a year, and one location can host several families. Unlike most other owls, barn owls don't mind nesting close together.

PJR-PHOTOGRAPHY/SHUTTERSTOCK.COM

poison to kill rodents may not realize the harm they are doing. They also may not know that they could deal with rodents without using killer chemicals.

Poison-free rodent control starts with rodent-proofing the problem site. That means blocking all entry points to buildings where rodents can find food and shelter, and getting rid of anything outside that they might eat. If there are still too many rodents around, their numbers can be reduced without resorting to poison. They can be tempted with a tasty bait containing ingredients that prevent them from having babies. They can also be dispatched with devices that kill instantly, such as snap traps or electronic zappers—but these devices must be used carefully so they don't harm other wildlife or pets.

If we want owls to do their job as rodent hunters, we need to welcome them into our neighborhoods and keep them safe. One of the leaders in the fight against secondhand wildlife poisoning is an organization called Raptors Are the Solution (RATS). It educates people about the dangers of rodent poisons and encourages them to switch to poison-free methods of rodent control. RATS is also working to make the widespread use of rodent poisons illegal.

TAKE ACTION: Download and print free posters, flyers and other educational materials from the RATS website and share them in your community. While you're on the website, check out the kids' page and watch *Raptor Blues*, a cool Claymation video made by a teenager.

WHO'S WHOO

RUSSELL BURDEN/GETTY IMAGES

Long-Eared Owl

When perched, long-eared owls have a Batman silhouette, but their ear tufts are barely visible in flight. These mainly nocturnal owls are found in many parts of the world north of the equator. They breed across much of the midsection of North America. In winter some travel to other parts of Canada and the United States and into Mexico. Long-eared owls nest and roost in places with lots of trees or shrubs and hunt in open areas such as grasslands, meadows, deserts and forest openings.

A short-eared owl flies across farm fields, carrying a rodent it has just killed. If farmers in the area are using poison to try to solve their rodent problems, this meal could be fatal for the owl.

Third-grade students at Central Boulevard Elementary School in Bethpage, NY, with two owl nests that their class made from vines and evergreen-tree branches. The nests were placed in trees in Bethpage State Park to encourage great horned owls to raise their families there.
THE BETHPAGE UNION FREE SCHOOL DISTRICT

A barred owl peeks over the edge of its doorway. Nest boxes should be made out of untreated, unpainted wood and have features like a sloped roof and drainage holes in the floor.
LASZLO PODOR/GETTY IMAGES

HOMES FOR OWLS

The holes owls nest in are mostly found in older trees that are decaying or dead. This type of home is getting harder to find in many places because so many suitable trees have been cut down. Wooden nest boxes can help make up for the loss of natural tree holes if they are designed properly and placed in the right kind of habitat. Owls that nest in tree holes like to be cozy, but they still need enough room to raise their families. They also prefer a doorway that is just big enough for the adults to squeeze through. A larger opening lets in more wind and rain and makes it easier for predators to invade.

Owls that most commonly use artificial nest boxes include eastern and western screech-owls, northern saw-whet owls, barred owls, boreal owls and barn owls. These species also use nest boxes for roosting. Good nest sites for great horned owls, great gray owls and long-eared owls are also in short supply in many areas. When these platform nesters can't find a suitable stick nest built by some other bird, they will often accept a nest basket made by weaving sticks into a wire-mesh cone lined with strong fabric.

TAKE ACTION: Put up an owl nest box or basket. You can find building plans and advice on the NestWatch website. You will need adult assistance for some parts of the construction and installation.

OWL SOS

What should you do if you come across an owl that seems to be in distress? First make sure it actually requires assistance. An adult owl may fly off awkwardly, land and then fly off again each time you get close. Remember, if it's breeding season the owl is probably faking an injury to distract you from its nest or young in case you're a predator. But an owl that's sitting on the ground and looks sleepy when you walk up to it definitely needs help. So does one showing visible signs of injury or illness—a damaged wing, leg or eye, blood on its body or difficulty breathing.

In any of those situations you should contact the closest wildlife rescue center. Staff there will tell you how to safely bring the owl to them or arrange for someone to come and get it. If there is no wildlife center nearby, contact a veterinarian. Don't try to look after a distressed owl on your own. It's illegal, and you may do more harm than good.

Wildlife rescue centers provide expert care for wild animals that are injured, sick or orphaned. Whenever possible, animals are returned to the wild once they are able to survive on their own. When they receive a new patient, staff members start by examining the animal just like a doctor would examine you. They may take blood samples or do an x-ray. Then they might have to do surgery or splint a broken bone. Some injured animals need pain pills, antibiotics to clear up an infection, or physiotherapy. However long it takes, the wildlife center will support the patient's recovery by giving it a quiet place to heal, proper food and loving care.

WHO'S WHOO

NPS/PUBLIC DOMAIN

Boreal Owl

Boreal owls live in the boreal forest all across North America and Eurasia. They also live in high mountain forests in western Canada and the United States. They depend on mature forests, where in winter the snow stays soft under the evergreen trees so they can plunge in and catch rodents. In summer this habitat provides plenty of tree holes for nesting and cool shade for roosting. These small owls are mainly nocturnal. Their legs and toes are covered with thick feathers that protect against winter cold.

TAKE ACTION: Hold a fundraiser for your local wildlife rescue center or a center dedicated to rescuing and rehabilitating owls and other raptors.

A northern pygmy-owl called Petey receives treatment for a broken wing at the Alaska Raptor Center. Once he had healed, Petey could fly again but not silently enough to hunt well. Instead of returning him to the wild, the center gave him a permanent home.
ALASKA RAPTOR CENTER

OWLETS ON THE GROUND

Fledglings of many owl species are poor fliers for days or weeks after they leave their nest. Sometimes people find them on the ground and think they are in trouble. If there is no adult owl in sight, they also might assume that a fledgling is an orphan. In reality, the parents are probably nearby and doing their job.

How can you tell if an owl is a fledgling? Its plumage will be a mix of feathers and fuzz because its adult feathers are still growing in. In most cases fledgling owls should just be left alone. But you should reach out to a wildlife rescue center in any of these situations:

- ► The owl is injured.

- ► The owl is in a dangerous location such as a road, a parking lot, the edge of a swimming pool or an area where dogs or cats are roaming loose.

- ► You are certain that both parents are dead.

You should also contact the rescue experts if you find an owlet that is a ball of fuzz or fluff with few or no real feathers. A youngster like that is most likely a nestling that has fallen out of its nest.

TO THE RESCUE

To pick up a sick, injured or orphaned owl and take it to a wildlife rescue center, work with an adult and follow these steps:

▶ Find a cardboard box that will comfortably hold the owl. Cut air holes into the sides, and line the bottom with an old (but clean) towel. Don't use a wire cage—it can damage the owl's feathers.

▶ Slowly approach the owl and cover it with a towel or jacket. This calms the owl and protects you. Watch for the owl's claws and beak, and press its wings against its body as you pick it up.

▶ Place the owl in the box and remove the covering used during the capture. Quickly close the lid and fasten it securely. Do not pet or touch the owl, because that will make it feel stressed. Do not give it anything to eat or drink.

▶ Keep the box in a warm, quiet, dark place away from pets and people until you're ready to go.

▶ When driving to the wildlife center, keep the radio off and talk as little as possible.

A young great horned owl that is being released sits on top of its carrier box. In a moment it will take flight. This orphan was cared for at a raptor rescue center until it was old enough to live independently.
CATHY WYATT/SHUTTERFAIRY PHOTOS

A burrowing owl at a wildlife center in Kamloops, BC.
CARLINA TETERIS/GETTY IMAGES

TAKE ACTION: Visit a raptor rescue center. Some are open to visitors year-round. Others hold a public open house once a year.

75

WHO'S WHOO

©JARED HOBBS

Snowy Owl

These Arctic owls are well insulated against the cold with dense, heavy plumage and thickly feathered legs, feet and face. They nest along the northern coasts of North America, Greenland and Eurasia. Most move south in winter. Where they go varies from year to year. Open, treeless areas across southern Canada and the northern United States are common destinations. During the continuous daylight of Arctic summer, snowy owls are active at all hours. In winter, down south, they are more nocturnal but are often seen sitting on fence posts, hay bales or other perches during the day.

Great gray owls are easiest to see in winter, when they often hunt during the day and sometimes roost on leafless treetops, poles or fence posts. Winter hunger and cold can make them sluggish and allow you to enjoy a long look. Remember to stay quiet and keep a respectful distance.

SHERI MINARDI PHOTOGRAPHY

PROWLING FOR OWLS

One of the easiest ways to show you give a hoot is by getting to know your local owls. Parks and nature centers often lead nighttime owl prowls. You can also organize your own owl prowl. Bring an adult with you if you're going to go anywhere beyond your own yard.

Owl prowls take a little preparation. First find out what kinds of owls live in your area and what habitats they prefer. Learn what the different species look and sound like. You will probably be using your ears more than your eyes to locate and identify owls.

Scout out your destination during the day so you can avoid stumbling and bumbling in the dark. When you go out at night, you will need to move slowly and quietly and talk only in whispers. Fast movements and loud noises can scare owls away before you even know they are there.

Wear sturdy shoes and dark clothing that won't rustle when you move. Dress warmly, because you will probably spend a lot of time standing still. If you have binoculars, bring them along. The moon and stars or the glow of city lights will usually brighten the sky enough to show the silhouettes of trees. Once you have tracked down an owl by its voice, binoculars will help you peer up into the branches to look for its dark shape.

You can go owl prowling throughout the year, but owlers usually have greatest success between late fall and early spring. That's when owls are most likely to be calling to declare their territories and attract mates. It's also easier to see them when branches are bare of leaves. Try to choose a clear, calm moonlit night. Owls are less active when it's windy or rainy, and if they do call, it's harder to hear them.

A short-eared owl glides across a sunset sky. If you are in an area where these owls live, try looking for them just as the sun is going down. In spring watch for sky-dancing males and listen for their wing claps.
SCOTT SURIANO/GETTY IMAGES

OWLING ETIQUETTE

Seeing owls in the wild is exciting. It's also a privilege. Owls are not out there for our entertainment. They're just going about their lives. Be a responsible and respectful owler by following these guidelines:

Give owls plenty of personal space. Observe from a distance. Use a telephoto lens if you want closeup pictures. Getting too close to roosting owls disturbs their sleep. Crowding them during their active period can keep them from hunting.

Back off if an owl shows any sign of stress—wide-eyed staring, fast blinking, sitting up very straight and skinny with its eyes reduced to slits and its ear tufts raised, rapidly looking around, fidgeting and panting.

Keep your distance from nests and limit your viewing time. Hanging around may prevent food deliveries or draw the attention of predators. Also keep in mind that owl parents are very protective. If they think you're a threat to their eggs or young, they may attack. Even a small owl's talons can inflict serious injuries.

Go easy on the owl calls. Most owls call back when they hear recorded or imitated calls. Often they will fly closer to check out the unfamiliar voice. Such reactions make it tempting to find owls this way. But dealing with too many phony calls wastes their energy and interrupts important activities like finding food, looking after their families or resting. Responsible owlers use recorded or imitated calls infrequently or not at all. They never use them to attract rare or endangered owls or in places that are visited by lots of owlers.

When owling in the dark, use your flashlight as little as possible, and never shine it directly at an owl. Bright lights interfere with the owl's night vision—and yours.

Leave your dog at home. Owls are afraid of dogs.

A great horned owl keeps close watch over its nest and nestling. Trespassers will not be tolerated.
©JARED HOBBS

OWLS AND US

About 30,000 years ago, someone scratched a portrait of an owl onto a soft rock wall deep inside a cave in southern France. The bird is 18 inches (45 centimeters) tall, has large ear tufts and is performing the unique owl trick of turning its head so far around that it seems to be put on backward. The drawing is one of the world's oldest surviving works of art. It shows that people have been fascinated by owls for a very long time. Our fascination is sure to continue as long as there are owls around. I hope that will be at least 30,000 more years.

MLORENZPHOTOGRAPHY/GETTY IMAGES

Some people think this 30,000-year-old rock art in Chauvet Cave in France shows a long-eared owl. Others say it's a Eurasian eagle-owl. Either way, the artist who went to the trouble of creating it clearly thought owls were important.

CLAUDE VALETTE/WIKIMEDIA COMMONS/CC BY-SA 4.0

Wild At Heart volunteer Danae Dearden stands in the bucket of an electricity company's lift truck with a young rescued barn owl. During this release she put owls into two treetop owl boxes—two in each one. She also popped in some frozen mice as a starter meal.

DAVID JOLKOVSKI/SEDONA RED ROCK NEWS

"I love the barn owls. They're so unique. They just look like little creepy vampires."

—Alora VanderVeen

OWL ALLIES

Taking Care of Rescued Owls

Wild At Heart is a raptor rescue, rehabilitation and release center in Arizona. This center cares for hundreds of owls, hawks, falcons and eagles every year. Most are eventually returned to the wild, but some never recover enough to be released. The permanent residents act as foster parents for rescued orphans and take part in educational programs.

Many wildlife centers rely on volunteers who assist the staff. Unlike most of them, Wild At Heart lets kids help out. Those who are 13 or younger start by teaming up with one of their parents. Once they are trained, they can come on their own.

The minimum age for volunteering at the center is normally 10, but Alora VanderVeen was only nine when she started in fifth grade. When I interviewed her she had been a Wild At Heart volunteer for four years.

Alora usually does weekly shifts of two to four hours. Her regular responsibilities include organizing and delivering meals and cleaning the aviaries where the birds live. "They fling food everywhere, so you have to scrub it off the walls," she says. She also sweeps up the pellets the birds spit up after eating and hoses the poop off their perches. Alora hopes to become a bird veterinarian, so she is always excited when she gets to assist the center's vet technician with tasks like bandaging wounds or giving laser-therapy treatments to help heal injuries.

Danae Dearden started volunteering at Wild At Heart when she was 12. She does many of the same jobs as Alora and has helped with some releases. Both girls also willingly tackle one task that many other volunteers prefer to avoid—cutting open the dead rodents and rabbits that are fed to the raptors and removing their guts. Danae plans to be a biologist and welcomes these opportunities to examine animal anatomy. "It ends up taking me forever because I find it really interesting," she says.

Danae and Alora both agree that being a raptor center volunteer is a great way to gain experience for a future career.

DAVID JOLKOVSKI/SEDONA RED ROCK NEWS

Alora VanderVeen with Mags, a great horned owl who came to Wild At Heart as a chick after falling from his nest. His head injuries left him partly blind. Nine years old in this picture, Mags lives in the center's clinic and is friendly with everyone.

TABITHA VANDERVEEN

Glossary

boreal forest—the type of forest that covers large parts of the northern regions of the North American, European and Asian continents and is made up of trees such as pine, spruce, larch, fir, poplar and birch

citizen scientists—people who do scientific research but are not professional scientists

clutch—a complete set of eggs laid by one bird

conservation—the preservation and protection of single species or whole ecosystems

crepuscular—active during the twilight period around dusk and dawn

diurnal—active in the daytime

duetting—the back-and-forth calling and singing between one male bird and one female bird

ear tufts—two bunches of longer feathers that sit on top of the head and that can be raised straight up or laid flat

ecosystem—a community of living things and the nonliving parts of their environment (such as water, soil and rocks), all linked together through nutrient cycles and energy flows

facial disk—a flattish circle of feathers that rings an owl's face

fledgling—a young bird that has recently left its nest

habitat—the place where a plant or animal makes its home and can get all the things it needs to survive, such as food, water and shelter

incubate—to keep an egg warm with body heat so the chick inside can develop

invertebrates—animals that have no backbone or spinal column

irruption—an irregular mass movement of birds to an area outside of their usual winter range

migration—regular long-distance travel back and forth between breeding grounds and wintering grounds

mobbing—noisy pestering of a bird such as an owl by a flock of other birds

nest boxes—wooden boxes built by people to provide nest sites for birds that normally nest in tree holes and other natural cavities

nestling—a young bird that is still living in its nest and being cared for by its parents

nocturnal—active at night

old-growth forest—a forest that has grown for a very long time without being disturbed by human activities, so it has many big old trees as well as younger trees growing up to eventually replace them

pellet—a small packet of undigested food that is compressed in the upper part of a bird's digestive system and spit back out

plumage—a bird's feathers

range—the entire area in which a species is found

raptors—birds of prey, including owls, eagles, hawks, falcons and kites

retina—the back part of the eye that contains light-sensitive cells called *rods* and *cones*

roost—the place where a bird sleeps or rests

roosting—sleeping or resting

species—a group of closely related organisms that have similar characteristics and can breed to produce offspring

talons—long, sharp claws

tundra—a vast area of flatland in the Arctic where it is too cold, dry and windy for trees to grow and the main plants are tough grasses, mosses, lichens and low shrubs

 # Resources

PRINT

Backhouse, Frances. *Owls of North America*. Firefly Books, 2008.

Berger, Cynthia. *Owls*. Stackpole Books, 2005.

Ford, Ansley Watson, and Denver W. Holt. *Snowy Owls, Whoo Are They?* Mountain Press Publishing Company, 2016.

Gove-Berg, Christie. *Greta The Great Horned Owl: A True Story of Rescue and Rehabilitation*. Adventure Publications, 2019.

Wilson, Mark Chester. *The Snowy Owl Scientist*. Clarion Books, 2022.

Yolen, Jane. *Owl Moon*. Philomel Books, 1987.

VIDEO

North Branch Nature Center. Saw-whet owl banding demonstration and discussion. northbranchnaturecenter.org/online/banding-station

Owl Research Institute. *Owl Notes*, five short films on Owl Research Institute projects. owlresearchinstitute.org/general-8

Ranger Rick, National Wildlife Federation. *William E. finds owl pellets*. rangerrick.org/nature/william-e-finds-owl-pellets-in-his-barn

Birds Canada Nocturnal Owl Survey:
birdscanada.org/bird-science/
nocturnal-owl-survey

Blakiston's Fish Owl Project: fishowls.com

eBird: ebird.org/about/resources/
for-young-birders

International Festival of Owls:
festivalofowls.com

International Owl Center:
internationalowlcenter.org

**International Wildlife Rehabilitation
Council (find a wildlife rehabilitator)**:
theiwrc.org/resources/emergency

**NestWatch (includes building plans for
owl boxes and baskets)**: nestwatch.
org/learn/all-about-birdhouses

Owling.com: owling.com

Owlproject.org: owlproject.org

Owl Research Institute:
owlresearchinstitute.org

The Poo-Poo Project: tetonraptorcenter.org/
poo-poo-project

Project SNOWstorm: projectsnowstorm.org

Raptors Are the Solution (RATS):
raptorsarethesolution.org

**US Fish and Wildlife Service feather
identification tool**:
fws.gov/lab/featheratlas/idtool.php

Wild At Heart raptor rescue center:
wildatheartraptors.org

**Wildwatch Burrowing Owl Zooniverse
project**: wildwatchburrowingowl.org

The World Owl Trust: owls.org

For a complete list of references, visit the page for this book at orcabook.com.

Links to external resources are for personal and/or educational use only and are provided in good faith without any express or implied warranty. There is no guarantee given as to the accuracy or currency of any individual item. The author and publisher provide links as a service to readers. This does not imply any endorsement by the author or publisher of any of the content accessed through these links.

A barred owl sits in a cedar tree, calmly observing a photographer below. If left in peace, it will soon go back to its daytime napping.

Acknowledgments

My first thank-you goes to all the biologists, citizen scientists, naturalists and Indigenous Knowledge Keepers whose owl expertise has contributed to my understanding and appreciation of these intriguing and important birds. In particular, I continue to be grateful to all those who helped me with my previous writing about owls, including several magazine articles and my adult book, *Owls of North America*, which laid the groundwork for this book.

This time around I was assisted in my text and photo research by Dave Alexander, Kristen Ballot, Karla Bloem, Leeza Chamberland, Richard Chamberland, Jennifer Cross, Anne Elliott, Charlotte England, Ange Grant, Adam Green, Stella Green, Jordan-Michael Hardey, Jonathan Haw, Anne Hayward, Jared Hobbs, Andrew Jakes, Greysen Jakes, Alex Jehle, Elsa Jehle, Mike Mackintosh, Amy McCarthy, Lauren Meads, Beth Mendelsohn, Sheri Minardi, Sara Orchardson, Amanda Penn, Emily Senninger, Jonathan Slaght, Lauren Smith, Melissa Sokolowski, Amy Steffian, Vishal Subramanyan, Michael Utecht, Scott Weidensaul, Malcolm Wilson, Kate Wright, Vicky Young and Daphne Yun. Thank you all.

Scott Weidensaul also graciously agreed to read my first draft and provided very helpful feedback. If there are any errors in the book, they are entirely mine.

An extra-big thank-you to the six inspiring young people who shared their owl experiences with me: Jaden Barney, Isabella Bishara, Danae Dearden, Emma Drake, Adivhaho Mokakatleng and Alora VanderVeen. Matching thanks to the people who made it possible for me to have those conversations: Liza Barney, Rena Dearden, Laura Drake, Beth Edwards, Jordan-Michael Hardey, Amy-Lee Kouwenberg, Gabby Vera, Tabitha VanderVeen and Motlatsi Zulu.

I'm grateful to everyone at Orca Book Publishers who supports my work, including those whose contributions happen out of my sight. I especially appreciate Kirstie Hudson's warmth, enthusiasm and fine editing skills.

On the home front, Mark Zuehlke offered his usual patient listening ear, wise counsel and sense of humor and put up with my often owlish work hours. Every author should be so lucky.

Index

*Page numbers in **bold** indicate an image caption.*

MARK ZUEHLKE

FRANCES BACKHOUSE studied biology in university and worked as a park naturalist and a biologist before becoming an environmental journalist and author. She is the award-winning author of *Beavers: Radical Rodents and Ecosystem Engineers* and *Grizzly Bears: Guardians of the Wilderness* in the Orca Wild series, as well as six books for adults, including *Owls of North America*. She lives in Victoria, British Columbia.